Praise for

Our Bones Ache Together

In six entrancing parts, Kendra Nuttall guides us gently through an intimate series of poems that sing with longing and dance with desire. *Our Bones Ache Together* pulls us through a myriad of seemingly quotidian experiences, with lines that engage, inspire, and excite. Kendra turns each moment in these verses into an insightful tug-of-war—the elegance of her verse juxtaposed brilliantly against the simplicity of the insights she delivers through each little 'story' she tells. It's like peering into a portrait of an inner life; thoughts, feelings, relationships, connections, emotions, all laid bare so readers can find their own anecdotes within verses that feel just familiar enough to be comforting, and just unfamiliar enough to fascinate and inspire.

—**Rhea Dhanbhoora**, author of *Sandalwood-Scented Skeletons*

Poetry of life knit together beautifully by a poet who meditates on all moments of existence whether seemingly mundane or eventful or the in between, then makes each and every one of them special with her unique craft of lyrical and profound writing.

—**Vaishali Paliwal**, author of *Water Bearer's Song*

In *Our Bones Ache Together*, Kendra Nuttall explores home, heartache, healing, and hope. She grapples with the emotional toll of losing your childhood home and learning to make a new home on your own. An all-too-familiar millennial anxiety runs through the poems: fending for yourself, feeling trapped, and questioning everything. But whatever the world throws at her, Kendra ultimately finds hope and comfort in her relationship with her husband, writing: "It was raining and we were happy. / It's raining and we are still happy." Kendra has an eye for vivid details that make her poems pop. She captures the grief of losing her father, of the recent elections, of moving on in short, economical poems—after all, in this economy, with the cost of living and housing prices and student loans, who can afford to waste words? Kendra Nuttall will break your heart with just a few words in *Our Bones Ache Together*.

—**Carolina VonKampen**, editor in chief of *Capsule Stories*

Our Bones Ache Together

FLOWERSONG
PRESS

Poems by
Kendra Nuttall

FLOWERSONG
PRESS

FlowerSong Press
Copyright © 2023 by Kendra Nuttall
ISBN: 978-1-953447-56-2
Library of Congress Control Number: 2022951919

Published by FlowerSong Press
in the United States of America.
www.flowersongpress.com

Cover Image:
"Pulling Together" by Amy Casey
https://www.amycaseypainting.com/2008

Cover Design by Kendra Nuttall
Set in Adobe Garamond Pro

NOTICE: SCHOOLS AND BUSINESSES
FlowerSong Press offers copies of this book at quantity discount with bulk
purchase for educational, business, or sales promotional use. For information,
please email the Publisher at info@flowersongpress.com.

For David,
there's no one else I'd rather quarantine with.

Contents

Part Four: Moving Out

Part Five: Movements

Part Six: Moving Forward

Our Bones Ache Together

Part One:
Moving In

Furniture

Our bones ache together
on cool autumn mornings.

We both wear blankets
disguising dirt.

You and I don't want to move,
but sometimes we have to.

Bidding War

They don't tell you that gambling happens
outside of Vegas, in every suburb,
every grandmother's azalea beds
and white picket fence:
twenty and thirty-somethings indebted
to student loans and tradition
attempting to buy their first home.

It's a war out there,
at least they told me that.
Now do the math.

It has potential.
It has good bones.
I have good bones too, but
that won't stop the bulldozer.
I have good bones too, but
your best bid is due at noon.

Apartment 460

There's nothing romantic about moving
in together. It's just nostalgia baking

in your birthday cake. We're twenty pounds
lighter and our stove is avocado green.

We have three guinea pigs, two part-time jobs,
and one infestation of boxelder bugs.

I'm learning that six-hundred square feet
is not enough in the aftermath of an argument

and six feet under is too much
for someone I love. And I love you, I do,

every day in the grocery store aisle,
in the heart of Timpanogos,

in the middle of the Caribbean Sea
on the deck of a cruise ship, I do.

There's nothing romantic about moving
in together. The romance is growing up

and getting old with you and our pets,
snoring next to me by the soft glow of the TV.

Apartment 12

I've just eaten three Ikea cinnamon rolls
and picked out furniture I can't afford

for this apartment we can't afford
in this city we can't afford, but the view

of the mountains from the dining room
window makes it all worth it. And hey,

at least we have a dining room.
People ask when we're going to have kids

and I ask if they actually care
about the environment.

The lawn is mowed every Tuesday
at seven, our poodle's paws are dyed

green every Tuesday at eight,
and we go to the office every day

from nine to five and think about life
before we thought about time,

when the grass grew slow and the hands
on the clock didn't spin out of control.

An Apology to Ugly

Boxelder bug vacuumed
up in search for November warmth.
November—harsh wind spreading
autumn's final moments across the sky.
The sky colored in sick gray,
moments before a winter storm.
Winter reminding us again and again
of time.

Everyone's immortal until they're not.
Even pretty things expire,
like the ladybug I let outside,
those invisible broken wings
falling from the third floor.
Who's to say the boxelder
shouldn't be saved?

My Neighbor the Hoarder is Dead

My new neighbors don't love each other.
I hear them through gossiping walls
and over insecure parking lots,
screaming sour nothings
for an audience of everyone.

They have a little girl.

Maybe she wants the world,
but she's stuck growing up
with TV dinner and left turns.
How lucky I am,

watching my Roomba
vacuum my cares away.
I'll dump them in the trash
where they'll become
another worry on top of a world's worth.

I don't even have to care.

Part Two:
Unmovable

Laugh Track

Don't run with scissors.
I shouldn't have to say

"don't run with scissors."
Pause for laughter.

My anger is as heavy as my hair
but I'm trying to be more positive,

trying to turn these baby blues
pink like my favorite security blanket.

It's sitting somewhere in storage
draped over childhood abandoned

for so-called cool; at least
my stuffed animals are secure

while I drift in and out of sleep
wishing I could still count sheep.

We're all victims
of growing up, just ask

the sitcom character
pausing for endless laughter.

Interior Design

There's calm in headaches,
like a winter hug, wind
bursting with morning sick.

I don't want to be Mom,
I already killed my Venus
fly trap with a cruel joke.

I've tried to stop the clock,
but where would I be
without the constant tick
of the bathroom faucet
reminding me nothing lasts

forever? I only open
calendars to see the pictures.
There's August,
sweet summer child,
sitting in her midcentury chair
made modern again.

Swimming Lessons

My chlorine dream
turned yellow

when the band-aid
brushed against my leg

like a shark.
The fear is real;

wounds stay wet
buried under security

blankets. And skin
sweats without reprieve

until the rip,
when eyes drip and

the shark circles back
toward public pools.

The Weight of Water

The person you love is 60% water.
I've never learned how to swim.

The weight of water is deceiving.
I've drowned in dreams

and bug-infested puddles.
I've drowned in diapered pools

and canyons as narrow
as a Republican's mind.

I've drowned in oceans
as vast as Jeff Bezos's pockets

and rivers as twisted
as dogs riding in truck beds.

You tell me how beautiful the lake is,
and all I see is shimmering concrete.

Last Name

Third place in the school spelling bee / bees dying in my curly hair / gel spell / misspelling / nut / *nuez* / English / land of nuts / "BuT yoU dOn't LoOK VenEzuElAn." / typo / "Why don't you take your husband's last name?" / paperwork and identity theft / Who am I? / 23 & Me / Adam & Eve / religious freedom / freedom from religion / pioneer / patriarchy / mother tongue

Brandy Melville Like

I'm fascinated by the accumulation of fat
clinging to my thighs like clouds,
like cotton candy, except   chafing.

I try to bike. These biker shorts don't fit.
My inner thigh says *close your seam*.
Remember when thigh gaps were a thing?

I'm frustrated by the accumulation of fat
clinging to my thighs like teenage depression.

I put on my best bra to attend the Zoom meeting.
I am five feet tall. My dog is taller.
Calories in. Calories out.
Calories.

I try not to count the stretch marks
multiplying like weeds.
        I try not to compare my body to weeds.

Part Three: Removable

Burnout

My childhood bathroom had brown carpet,
twenty years of stains embedded in the fibers
under my bare feet. It didn't bother me then.

Tonight, I'm lying awake on a motel mattress,
searching for stars hidden somewhere
beyond the city lights.

I haven't seen them in years.

How many people slept in these sheets?
How many hands touched these towels?
How many feet scraped across this carpet?

You could vacuum and scrub and never erase
all the memories and skeletons and dirt
trapped inside these four walls.

We tore out the bathroom carpet
when it came time to sell the house,
but there's no hiding behind a remodel.

Every home has its secrets.
Every star burns out.

Christmas Eve

I'm sitting in front of the muted TV
watching images flash across the screen —

Channel 2 News making poinsettia bouquets,
Clark Griswold carving the Christmas turkey,

lips moving in frenetic silence.
I'm listening for the hum of my father's snores

to know that he's still breathing.
To know that he's still alive.

It's always winter here.
This house never catches the sun in time.

My father's frail body is unrecognizable
under a flurry of fleece, his face

the color of day-old snow. To think,
he was the man who sang at my wedding

only three months ago. It was winter then too,
we just didn't see the frost written in the lawn.

We never do, until no blanket can
capture the warmth we crave.

Capernaum Road

What I hate most about swimming
is getting out of the pool —
unsticking soggy swimsuit from skin,
shivering waddles in sloshing flip-flops,
eating sandwiches with pruned fingers,
cold water dripping from damp hair,
all the while surrounded
by the stench of chlorine and hint of pee.

This is to say, my childhood bathroom had carpet.
This is to say, I don't trust boomers.

My childhood home had an unfinished basement
I was afraid of and a backyard with raspberry bushes.
My childhood home had a bright turquoise bedroom
and a broken orange tile.
My childhood home had a peeling red deck
and couch held together by duct tape.

My childhood home is listed on Zillow,
sterile and staged like a furniture showroom.
They've gone for a modern farmhouse look,
popular with every suburban family.
I'm sure it will sell quick, after all,
location, location, location,

yet I can't help but remember
what Christmas morning looked like
in the living room when my childhood home was lived in.

Birdwatching at Mystic Hot Springs

I've never come close to being
a mother, but I feel maternal

watching the mama bird fly
in and out of the nest, dropping crickets

and berries as her babies cry
and crowd together for dinner.

I look away as they edge closer to the cliff,
nothing but waterlogged rocks below.

I want to catch and comfort them
after the inevitable fall,

but there's a cliff next to me too.

The Middle Class Is

welcome mat
holiday wreath
holiday
Costco hot dog
Costco
walk-in closet
home office
three queen-sized beds:
       happy marriage
       future wife
       future tech guy
dog house with real bones
dog
family breakfast on Friday mornings
(feels) clean on Friday nights
clothes shrinking in the laundry.

Seasons Change, but the Décor Stays the Same

I don't have storage space,
what am I, a billionaire?

I get my inspiration in the aisles
of HomeGoods. Those home gods,

with their feather lamps and fake plants
give me all the oxygen. I don't breathe

real trees. My office doesn't have windows.
I know, I know, *be grateful*

you have an office. My kids haven't
shut up for six months. I have a dog.

I like dogs. I have nothing to write about
except dogs — she's my blanket, my mop,

my high blood pressure. I'm having
pizza for dinner. It's not the same

without checkered tablecloths
and mood lighting, so I sit with the dark,

pour a glass of wine, and
reach down to pet my dog.

Part Four:
Moving Out

Honey Bear

I'm finding the gap   between the stove and counter
for the first time.
Like a forgotten spam folder,

everything is piling up.
Walmart receipts in my front seat;
dust bunnies reminding me
of the guinea pigs I gave away;
hair clumps from the cat I didn't hold
as she went to sleep for the last time.

I say I don't care
about the high school yearbooks, but
here they are packed into boxes
      again.

I say I'm ready to move on,
but how much stuff
can one really fit into a box?
How many licks does it take
to get to the center of a tootsie
pop?

I don't like tootsie pops.
I don't like tootsie rolls.
I like *Tootsie* and Jessica Lange.
Who doesn't like Jessica Lange?
I digress.

There's a bear-shaped jar of honey
sitting on the counter next to the gap.

If food could talk,
which I'm glad it cannot,
Honey Bear would say
you're going to be okay,

and maybe that would be enough.

Speed Trap Ahead

I'm afraid of driving
because I don't trust.

I don't trust the construction
cones sitting lonely
like they have every day
for five years, begging
to embrace.

I don't trust the minivan
mom swerving
during this week's sixth
cereal incident.

I don't trust the dad-bodied
man behind the wheel of the RV,
driving for the first time
this decade; he thinks
his so-called semi-truck sized
[redacted] belongs in the fast lane.

I don't trust the teen driver.
Who does?

I don't trust cops.
Even Google Maps doesn't.
"Speed trap ahead."
I am already trapped.

I Visit the Met Before the World Ends

The world ends every day since it began; it ends
as two cars collide in a violent dance,
as two lovers close their eyes, one for the final time.
It ends on Titanic and in towers I'm too young
to remember,   in bombs no one told me
my country dropped.
It ends in emergency room wails
and school playground scrapes.
It ends on Monday morning and election night.
It ends every winter
when I lose my father again.
It ends where flames engulf forests and hurricanes
lose paradise.
It ends as Van Gogh paints another self-portrait alone.
It ends in Pompeii and Sandy Hook, in Holocaust and ventilator hum,
in war after war after war   never peace.
It ends in an Egyptian tomb in New York and in the Garden of Eden
where Eve is deceived by a man the first time,
if only it was the last.

At Least After the Apocalypse

We'll still have Subway.
We'll always have Subway
in seedy gas stations,
on stairways to heaven,
in our dreams, our nightmares,
our half-baked brains.
I'm not twenty-five, I can't
rent a car but I can live I can die
I can.
My uncle says he likes flying.
He doesn't remember security.
He doesn't remember sleeping
with a fifteen-dollar sandwich,
red-eyed, damning damn red-eye flights.
I ask the TSA agent for the hundredth time,

      why?

Why is anything does anything
am anything are anything 44,758 Subways
nothing.

St. George Island in September

The leaves back home are turning tangerine
like a monarch's wings under wildfire skies.
They stop here before migrating south, as I do
before migrating back to 24-hour news cycles
and idling traffic. On the island,
palm trees sway to never-ending reggae,
oblivious to impending winter.
On the island, the ocean is always crystal,
and I'm not talking about the meth lab
that lit up last week. On the island,
we are nowhere and we are everywhere.
On the island, I am midnight sea turtle tracks
and ghost crab. On the island,
I am morning thunder and gold lightning.

I watch a monarch skating
over the sea, deceived by postcard perfection.
The battering ram hits,
and the butterfly flutters one last time
before its skeleton settles in the sand.
Did you know seashells are skeletons too?
The beach is a cemetery and sanctuary,
the ocean a murder mystery,
the island yesterday, today, and tomorrow.

Don't Feed the Ducks

says the sign,
but toddlers can't read; they only toddle.
Their parents can read but would rather not.

Therefore, our neighborhood pond's once polite
ducks are now plump and happy to stalk
innocent anglers for bread.

There's one duck, however,   (call him ugly duckling if you need a fairytale)
who doesn't follow
the zombied flock. I watch him limp

towards the shade of a tree, alone,
abandoned, resigned to his fate of unfavorite.
Every time I think of the cruelty of humans

I remember our animal friends aren't always nicer,
though they're far more cute. At least I know
if I were hurt, a doctor would take care of me (for a fee.)

If I were hurt,
you'd be there with breakfast
to help me feel better.

If I were hurt,
I wouldn't be alone,
no matter how lonely pain can be.

Watermelon Cliffs

Do national parks ever feel lonely?
Look at Capitol Reef, alone in the desert,
as lovely as any cowboy cliché, her hoodoos
and arches forming in their first trimester
against a backdrop of red.

Have you ever met a child
you knew would grow up to do great things?
She practices piano every day,
makes the honor roll each semester, but
never makes friends.

I wonder who's in charge of marketing
for Capitol Reef. If it were up to me,
I'd call it Watermelon Cliffs
for the sunset streaks blushing the rock
and electric green trees dressing its sides.

But what do I know about marketing?
What do I know about loneliness?
I know that desert dreams are a dime a dozen.
I know that time goes by too slow on the road
and too fast running against the edge of a cliff.

Where Hairlines Go to Die

I don't have cable, but I
binge *90 Day Fiancé* wherever I can,
stupid Americans in stupid airports
picking up love,
I can't get enough.
I'm moving to Cambodia and telling everybody
I'm grieving and lost.
      For sure,
I buried my father under six feet of Idaho,
but, truth is, I'm a little bored too.
The mountains aren't majestic enough
and Californians are clogging the roads and
this concrete cubicle is where hairlines go to die.
I want new car smell. I want Eat, *Prey*, Love. I want *Toxic*
by Britney Spears. I want more than 55%.
Give me expensive words, give me the best of the best.
I need Zied to tell me he loves me *so much*.
I need a pep talk from Darcey, a hug from Armando,
Annie's Thai food, Libby's Moldovan wedding
with all the bread and beyond,
gimme more gimme more gimme more,
but the world is an abusive relationship.
It's Angela's cigarettes.
It's Colt's dick pics and Deavan's selfies.
Will we still care in ten years?
Will you read this in ten years?
      I remember the day I landed in Seattle,
how beautiful the trees were. I could get lost.
      I remember the day my aunt came to Utah;
look how beautiful those mountains are.
      I remember the day I set foot in Cambodia
and finally understood.

While Walking My Dog in Utah County
on a Thursday Afternoon

I watch her press into the macabre perfume
of a baby bird's corpse and think, *now you need a bath.*

That is my first thought. Not *how sad.* Not *poor thing.*
Not *bless you.* There are too many achoos anyway.

I've become immune to corpses.
I've become immune to wasps

hovering around the apartment complex pool.
I know how complex life is.

There are too many I's and not enough you's,
but the reality of this reality show life is that

we have to
choose.

Part Five:
Movements

Border

Who owns the earth
and who draws the borders?
I asked a question
and no one answered
until I crossed the line.

Genocide Alphabetized

Aboriginal, Acholi, Aché, American, Armenian, Assyrian, Bihari, Bosnian, Buddhist, Cambodian, Chechen, Chinese, Christian, Circassian, Communist, Cossack, Crimean, Darfur, Disabled, French, Greek, Haitian, Herero, Hindu, Homosexual, Hutu, Igbo, Indonesian, Intellectual, Irish, Isaaq, Jew, Kazakh, Kurd, Lango, Latvian, Libyan, Mapuche, Mayan, Moriori, Muslim, Nama, Ndebele, Papuan, Polish, Pygmy, Rohingya, Romani, Rwandan, Selk'nam, Serbian, Shia, Sikh, Tibetan, Ukrainian, Uyghur, Yanomami, Yaquis, Yazidis, Zunghar.*

* The definition of genocide, according to Oxford, is the deliberate killing of a large group of people. As deliberate killings of large groups of people occur daily, this list is by no means comprehensive. If it were, you would read forever.

** Many genocides are known by different names, depending on whose side you're on.

*** Many genocides overlap with other genocides, like different foods touching on plates.

**** Some genocides may refer to multiple genocides, for example, the American Genocide may refer to:
1. The deliberate killing of Native American tribes by European settlers.
2. The deliberate killing of Black people by law enforcement officers.
3. The deliberate killing of migrants by U.S. Border Patrol.
    And more.

***** The only continent unaffected by genocide is Antarctica, unless you count the deliberate killing of penguins via the deliberate ignoring of climate change.

Born in the USA (2020)

It's almost the Fourth of July,
but it feels like the day after Valentine's

when all the candy hearts are discarded
and the snow hits harder than ever, as if

God is angry I didn't get him a Valentine.
I watch tanks take my city and think of Tiananmen.

I watch a president praise God.
God, whose side are you on?

I drink beer that tastes like summer 2016
when my biggest concern was fitting into jeans.

2016, my dad's cancer diagnosis.
2016, my mom went home to Venezuela

to say goodbye. 2016, presidential election.
Hindsight is 2020. Maybe our clichés cursed

the decade. There used to be a rumor in the family
that my mom married my dad for a green card.

I watch an old man shuffle across the TV screen
and think *run*. Police push him to the ground.

Later, I'll find out he has leukemia. The police
are looking into the police. *Wink wink.*

I paint a white doll brown. I remember when
my *abuelita* made me a doll. I remember when

a girl called my Black Barbie ugly. I remember when
she said my curly hair looked better straight.

I remember when the police helped
my crying mom after the car wreck.

I remember our next-door neighbor, the cop
with a son my age. We were never good friends.

Born in the USA plays on the radio.
I picture patriots singing along and I wonder

if they listen to every word as fireworks light the night.
Got nowhere to run, ain't got nowhere to go.

Eight minutes and forty-six seconds feels like forever
trapped under the weight of the elephant in the room.

On Second Thought

I'm sorry
to the wasp splayed
against our bedroom window
like a museum display.
It's still alive, occasionally
twinging with hope.
You tell me wasps don't have hope.
You tell me wasps don't feel pain.
We're both too afraid to kill it.

I know the cruelty of humans.
I've seen too many dogs
holding on
in the back of a pickup truck,
never losing trust.
I've seen innocent men
thrown to the ground,
and no one even stops to form
a first thought.

My America

Pre-packaged sodium-laced salad in plastic wrap.

Fake news, Fox News, Facebook.

Flag bumper sticker, flag t-shirt, flag coffee mug, flag bikini, flag
tablecloth,
                but don't you dare throw the flag on the floor.

I pledge allegiance to tradition: apple pie/baseball/school shootings.

A bible you never read
        and a poetry section shoved to the back of the store.

Sixteen-year-old with solo cup.
Sixteen-year-old dreams of being CEO.
Sixteen-year-old has no health insurance.

Life, liberty, and the pursuit of Black people.

Land of the free, home of the brave, let me translate:
Land of for-profit prisons, home of the brave.

White and blue,
        red for you.

Inspiration Point

Most moments, I doubt
God's existence, such as

when I see a single orange cone
overturned in the middle of a country road,

and I think, who put you here? And
who left you here?

There are moments when I also think maybe
God just likes to lay low, lets us bask

in the majesty of creation to make us
go back to church

before he takes our toys away.
This is one of those moments:

Bryce Canyon is my toy box.
Its tangerine hoodoos are my building blocks.

I'll build and I'll build
my tower of Babel

until I can talk to God
hiding somewhere among the bristlecone pines,

vermillion cliffs,
and Milky Way.

Where We're Going

American is not a religion, but bible
verses are written on our soda cups.

God is In-N-Out / is Forever 21 / is a roadside
billboard somewhere south of Normal,

Illinois. *Where are you going?*
Heaven or Hell? The anti-masker says

I'm going to hell. Politics are not a sport,
but team spirit is what keeps us alive.

My neighbor, #blessherheart, wrote:
#coronavirusruinslives in response to:

"My fav all u can eat place
isn't doing all u can eat anymore."

I want to tell her what it's like to lose
someone you love. It's like a buffet

shutting down, but forever.
It's like a pandemic, but permanent.

It's like the suffocating heat of a mask,
but you can never get rid of the sweat.

I want to tell her #coronaviruskills
but the message will never make it through

our socially distanced feeds.
American is a religion, politics are sport,

and we're on opposite teams.
Where are you going?

Innocence

Even the most innocent creatures can learn pain.
A dog will bite and love at the same time.

We forgive them, how could we not? Just look at those

     sad eyes,

but when it's time to forgive ourselves,
whose eyes will we see?

Part Six:
Moving Forward

Justice for Sunshine

We could wash the graffiti
off, but the fence in front of
the RV lot won't be any prettier
and the salesmen will never
stop selling dreams.

I'm afraid if we wash it away,
we'll forget the feeling of
Saturday afternoon.
Porch swings and laughter,
green trees stretching
above us for miles and miles.
That's what sunshine does,
coats everything in smiles

until golden hour
when romance comes alive.
How it flashes and shines.
How it dances and dives into blue

     sadness.

It's too quiet at night.
Too lonely, too dark.
Moonlight tries its best,
but it withers and wanes,
disappears to meet the sun
wherever she sleeps.

We need her,
the sun and her beams,
blooming petals haloing
the 7-Eleven,

the auto shop,
the apartment,
the fence in front of the RV lot
where Justice for Sunshine cries.

We could wash it off, but we won't.

12 Observations While Hiking

1. At some point, graffiti turns into history.
2. Rattlesnakes are anti-social.
3. Fellow hikers only say hi if you make eye contact.
4. Don't make eye contact.
5. Little dogs have something to prove.
6. Big men have something to prove.
7. Squirrels are adorable.
8. Stretching is important.
9. Sunscreen is important.
10. I will never be able to run up a mountain.
11. Will I ever be history?
12. I wonder.

Sunday Evening in Happy Valley

On the mountain by my house,
there's a daisy buffet for hardworking hoverflies
and busy bees. I picnic with my poodle
as she picks apart logs and picks risk
by poking her head into empty
rattlesnake dens.

I watch the pollinators partake of their nectar sacrament
as the churchgoers below partake of theirs and I partake
of mine. I can see the steeples from here, a hundred little dots;

a flaming sun setting into flamingo, haloing my hymn.

And heaven and nature sing.
And heaven and nature eat.

Love Poem Number 1

I want to write about my lover,
but I don't like the word lover
and I don't know how to describe love.
He's afraid of heights and so am I,
though a different kind.
I take his hand,
summer sun beating down
the edge of the cliff.
Our palms are sweaty,
feet gently pushing red
rocks and sand
to the ancient bed below.
I don't know if any god exists,
but I know there is something
strong enough
to carve cathedrals out of canyons,
to make stained glass out of sunsets,
to sing summer and cry winter,
to bring spring out of dead things.
My love's eyes are closed
and I want him to see this,
so I take a picture
to save for tomorrow
and we turn back home.

David

1.

David is everywhere:
in the classroom, in the office,
in my house, in my head,
sipping coffee incessantly,
on the sidewalk jogging shirtless,
in the Prius looking smug,
in the Ford spilling sauce,
eating Chick-fil-A (for the sauce, not the politics),
on the TV screen — both interviewer and interviewee,
in court — both judge and jury,
in park as owner,
in park as dog,
nickname: Dave,
AKA Grilling Master,
AKA World's #1 Dad,
AKA Mr. Cool.

2.

David Arquette
David Beckham
David Bowie
David Carradine
David Copperfield
David Duchovny
David Foster Wallace
David Hasselhoff
David Lee Roth
David Letterman
David Morrissey
David Ortiz

David Schwimmer
David Sedaris
David Spade
David Tennant
David, slayer of Goliath.

3.

David is 5 feet and 11.5 inches tall.
He is usually white.
He is lactose intolerant, but cheese pizza is life.
The Office is his favorite TV show.
Check out his podcast.

4.

I have a few David's of my own:
David, the target of elementary school bullying.
David, everyone's boyfriend at some point or another.
David, the conservative lawyer who reminds me of my father.
David, the Target cashier.
David, my YA novel protagonist.
David, 1 in 28 Americans.
David, my husband.

During Pandemics Everyone Writes About the Sky

Sun rays against skin, birds chasing half-empty airplanes
across mango sunsets into moonlight.

I remember the Idaho sky in fall.
I remember Grandpa's Thanksgiving Day hugs.
I remember Thanksgiving.

I'm one of the lucky ones, I haven't forgotten
touch. I haven't forgotten the impossible
warmth radiating from sleeping dogs on winter mornings.

I haven't forgotten
how to feel. Do you remember the day we got married?
It was raining and we were happy.
It's raining and we are still happy.

Balcony

From the mismatched neon and pastel patio
collecting cobwebs, to custom-made
cherry chairs that will never be sat in
and Ikea tables holding memories
of family reunions and arguments
echoing across the complex,
every balcony tells a story.

A woman smokes her fourth cigarette.
A man dances to blaring reggaeton.
The smell of stir-fry wafts from an open window.
The siren sound of political talk wails from another.

It's an election year.
We're no longer neighbors,
but players on opposing teams
and we know who thinks they're most special
based on the size of their flags.

We forget by Christmas
when lights are strung
on railings shining red and blue.

On New Year's,
the balconies are bare,
like newborns
emerging into a world of quiet snow.

Sometimes we forget to put the furniture back.

Kamala Harris Becomes Vice President and I Watch Real Housewives of Salt Lake City

Representation matters as she takes center stage
in silk, culmination of dream after dream after dream,

offering the stripped skin of my lips some much-needed
respite. I can finally sleep.

It's a new era
and my city is on TV,

draped in snowcapped mountains and labels
disguised as designer.

Reality shows are much better when left on screen.
I'll take an iceberg lettuce personality for president

if it means red cabbage stays trapped inside
my television (I rest my) case.

Kamala is a Housewife.
She doesn't ask to be heard.

Melania is a Housewife.
She really doesn't care, do you?

Hillary is a Housewife.
She fights and forgives.

Michelle is a Housewife.
When they go low, she goes high.

We are all Housewives.
We yell, we love, we cry.

We are all a little plastic
(literally, it's in our food).

We are all a little nasty
like Monday mornings.

We all need an escape
on Sunday nights.

Lift the Zion curtain at 11:30am
and let us into your heart.

Demi Lovato Sings at the Grammys

See John 11:35.

Is it a tear or a universe?

Why do I hurt.

When Lizzo nodded.

The A/C is broken.

My dog knows.

Dogs know everything.

The A/C broke a long time ago.

The universe is still here.

Jesus wept.

Remodel

These walls are my walls
to cover and paint,
to break and remake
as many times as it takes.

ACKNOWLEDGMENTS

Thank you to the editors of the following journals in which several of these poems, or earlier versions, first appeared:

Anti-Heroin Chic (2020): "Honey Bear", "Interior Design."

Capsule Stories (Winter 2020): "Burnout", "Christmas Eve."

Echolocation (2022): "Where Hairlines Go to Die."

Fleas on the Dog (Fall 2020): "12 Observations While Hiking", "Bidding War", "Capernaum Road", "David", "Don't Feed the Ducks."

Global Poemic (2020): "While Walking My Dog in Utah County on a Thursday."

Good Cop/Bad Cop Anthology (2021): "Genocide Alphabetized", "My America."

Hear Her Speak (2020): "Brandy Melville Like."

Sad Girl Review (2021): "Demi Lovato Sings at the Grammys"

Trouvaille Review (2020): "Birdwatching at Mystic Hot Springs."

What Rough Beast (2020): "Where We're Going."

AUTHOR BIO

Kendra Nuttall is a copywriter by day and poet by night. She is the author of poetry collection, *A Statistical Study of Randomness* (Finishing Line Press, 2021). Her work has been nominated for Best of the Net and has appeared in *Spectrum*, *Echolocation*, *Capsule Stories*, and more. She earned her BA in English from Utah Valley University (UVU) in 2018. Kendra was a first-place poetry winner in UVU's *Touchstones* journal and a presenter and winner at UVU's 2019 Showcase Awards.

Kendra lives in Utah with her husband and pets. When she's not writing, you can find her hiking, watching reality TV, or attempting to pet every animal she sees. Find her online at kendranuttall.com.